W9-CAD-094

WARRIORS OF HISTORY

SAMURAI

by Caroline Leavitt

Consultant:
Marcus Willensky
Director
International Research Department
FORMULATION K.K., Japan

Capstone press

Mankato, Minnesota

Edge Books are published by Capstone Press,
151 Good Counsel Drive, P.O. Box 669, Mankato, Minnesota 56002.
www.capstonepress.com

Library of Congress Cataloging-in-Publication Data
Leavitt, Caroline.
  Samurai / by Caroline Leavitt
  p. cm.—(Edge Books. Warriors of History)
  ISBN-13: 978-0-7368-6433-6 (hardcover)
  ISBN-10: 0-7368-6433-4 (hardcover)
  1. Samurai—History—Juvenile literature. 2. Japan—History—To 1868—Juvenile
literature. I. Title. II. Series.
DS827.S3L43 2007
952'.025088355—dc22   2005034936

Summary: Describes the Samurai, including their history, weapons, and way of life.

Editorial Credits

Mandy Robbins, editor; Thomas Emery, designer; Cynthia Martin, illustrator;
    Kim Brown, production artist; Jo Miller, photo researcher; Scott Thoms,
    photo editor

Photo Credits

Art Directors/Tibor Bognar, 28
Art Resource, NY/Alinari, 12; HIP, 23; Réunion des Musées Nationaux, 27;
    Werner Forman, 8
The Bridgeman Art Library/Fitzwilliam Museum/University of Chambridge, UK, 15
Corbis/Asian Art & Archaeology Inc., 9, 19; Bettmann, 10; Burstein
    Collection, 20–21; Earl & Nazima Kowall, 24; Stapleton Collection, 7
Getty Images Inc./Stone/Erik Von Weber, cover; Taxi/Tibor Bognar, 4
The Granger Collection, New York, 13, 16, 25
Mary Evans Picture Library, 18
SuperStock/Culver Pictures, Inc., 26

1 2 3 4 5 6 11 10 09 08 07 06

TABLE OF CONTENTS

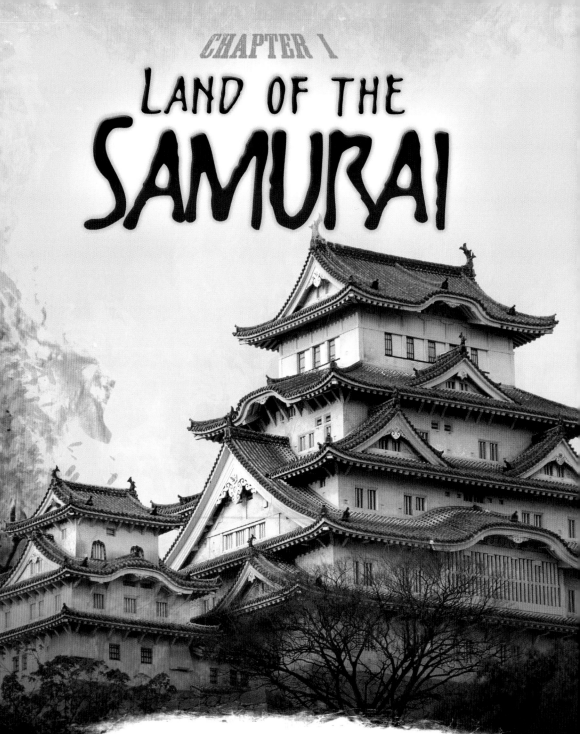

CHAPTER 1
LAND OF THE
SAMURAI

Japanese rulers, called daimyo, often lived in majestic castles that overlooked their land.

For thousands of years, the islands of Japan were cut off from the rest of the world. Among towering mountains and swampy rice fields, the Japanese created their own way of life.

About 1,000 years ago, Japan was made up of many small states. The emperor was the official ruler of Japan. But fierce noblemen called daimyo controlled the states. Owning land and rice fields made the daimyo very powerful. All of the people living on a daimyo's land obeyed him.

FIGHTING BEGINS

Daimyo needed help protecting their property and taking over new lands. They hired warriors to help them. The warriors were called samurai, which means "to serve."

LEARN ABOUT:
- Ancient Japan
- Powerful clans
- Emperors and shoguns

Daimyo and their extended families were called clans. Enemy clans fought one another for land and power. Two of the most powerful clans were the Minamoto and the Taira. They fought a war that began in 1180 and lasted five years. Eventually, the Minamoto won.

In 1192, the emperor made Yoritomo Minamoto Japan's first shogun, or general. As shogun, Minamoto had control over the emperor's samurai. This military control gave him more power than the emperor himself.

Europeans had no idea what Japanese people were like. This portrait of the Emperor Kogon, painted by a European artist, is completely inaccurate.

The Minamoto victory did not stop clans
from fighting. Other daimyo wanted to replace
Minamoto as shogun. By the mid 1500s, samurai
were constantly fighting for their daimyo. Respect
for the samurai grew as these great warriors
carved out their place in Japanese history.

新形三十六怪撰

大物之浦之雲
平家亡霊出現之嵪

According to legend, ghosts of defeated
Taira warriors haunt the seas off the

CHAPTER II
GREAT WARRIORS

LEARN ABOUT:
- Becoming a warrior
- Wandering samurai
- Living by the code

Samurai were the heroes of ancient Japan.

Samurai were greatly rewarded for their service. Daimyo gave their samurai grand homes, land, and money. Samurai were also the only people in Japan allowed to wear swords.

Becoming a samurai was easier for some people than for others. A boy born into a samurai family could easily follow in his father's footsteps. For those who weren't born into the warrior class, it was much more difficult. Before 1591, a man could prove himself by challenging and defeating a samurai. But in 1591, the shogun made it illegal for people of other classes to become samurai.

DIFFERENT TYPES OF SAMURAI

Daimyo had samurai perform different jobs. Housemen helped run the government instead of fighting. Fighting samurai were split into two groups. The first group was skilled in fighting on horseback. The other group fought on foot.

If a samurai left his master, or if his master died, he became a ronin. This means a "wave man." Ronin were called wave men because they wandered like waves in the sea.

No matter what job a samurai had, they all had the right to wear swords.

They had no master to give them food, shelter, or clothing. Some ronin worked odd jobs wherever they could find them. Lucky ronin found new masters to work for.

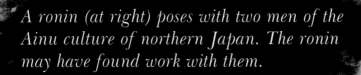

A ronin (at right) poses with two men of the Ainu culture of northern Japan. The ronin may have found work with them.

THE CODE OF BUSHIDO

Samurai lived by a set of rules called the code of bushido. Bushido means "the way of the warrior." This code controlled every part of a samurai's life.

According to the code, a samurai had to have unquestioning loyalty to his master. He must be willing to fight and die for him. Dying on the battlefield was considered an honor.

When they weren't fighting, samurai led simple lives. They tended their gardens and wrote poems. Samurai also meditated to clear their minds of war.

In daily life, a samurai had to be polite, honest, and self-disciplined. When a samurai gave his word, it was a firm promise.

Before going into battle, many samurai wrote poems about the possibility of being killed.

CHAPTER III

SAMURAI WEAPONS

LEARN ABOUT:
- Bows and arrows
- Importance of *swords*
- *Unlikely weapons*

Many high-ranking samurai wore helmets with a horned crest on them.

A samurai's first line of defense was his armor. Samurai armor was meant to terrify the enemy. Made of leather or metal, armor covered nearly the entire body. A samurai's armor made him appear much larger than he really was. Helmets looked like demons or animals about to attack.

BOWS AND ARROWS

The first samurai warriors fought on horseback, using bows and arrows. This was called "the way of the horse and bow."

Bows, made of wood or bamboo, were about 8 feet (2.4 meters) long. Arrows were measured using fists and fingers. They could be as long as 23 fists! That was about the same length as the bow. Sometimes samurai hollowed out their arrows. Hollow arrows made a frightening whistling sound as they whizzed by.

THE TREASURED WEAPON

Over time, some samurai began to rely more on their swords than bows and arrows. They carried both a long and a short sword. Samurai loved their swords. They often decorated them and gave them names.

The famous Japanese samurai Yashitsune was so skilled, he could use a fan as a weapon.

Though some samurai gave up their bows and arrows, they did not give up their horses. A warrior on horseback had a great advantage over a warrior on foot.

Samurai collected the heads of their enemies in battle. A polite samurai burned incense in his helmet to leave a pleasant smell for the enemy who took his head.

Aside from swords and bows and arrows, samurai had other unique weapons. They used spears called naginatas and a folding steel fan called a tessen.

A samurai's greatest weapon was his mind. If an enemy pulled back at nightfall, that's when the samurai would attack. Samurai also mastered martial arts. They could tell what moves their enemy might make and quickly stop them.

Even a samurai's breath could be a weapon. Before battle, a samurai prepared himself mentally by meditating. Slowly breathing in and out put his mind and body at peace. Before a samurai went into battle, he wanted to calmly accept the possibility of death.

Mask
Samurai wore masks to frighten their enemies.

Helmet
Looking into another man's helmet was considered a grave insult.

Armor
A suit of samurai armor usually weighed about 25 pounds (11 kilograms).

Wakizashi
This short sword was used for rituals.

Katana
This sword was the samurai warrior's long sword and was used most often in battle.

BATTLE BEGINS

Before a battle, the two sides faced each other about 300 feet (90 meters) apart. Commanders watched their troops from a hilltop. The battle began with the wave of a baton or fan.

Then, samurai horsemen charged into battle, followed by archers and spearmen. The thunder of galloping horses and battle cries filled the air. Above the noise, a samurai shouted his family name and rank, looking for an equal to fight.

The Heiji scroll records important events in Japan's history. One samurai battle recorded is the Heiji Insurrection of 1159.

CHAPTER IV

THE END OF THE
SAMURAI

LEARN ABOUT:

- *New weapons*
- *Japan in isolation*
- *The last samurai*

The first guns only fired one shot before needing to be reloaded.

In 1543, Europeans introduced the Japanese to some of the first firearms. The samurai quickly learned how to use the new weapons. By the end of the 1500s, Japan was creating some of the finest guns in the world.

But Japan's leaders worried about ordinary citizens having guns. Using guns, people with little fighting skill could rebel against the government.

From 1603 to 1867, Japan was ruled by the iron hand of the Tokugawa family. By 1725, Tokugawa shoguns had forced all foreigners out of Japan. They had also outlawed trade with other countries and banned all guns.

For about 250 years, Japan enjoyed peace and isolation. But the rest of the world was changing fast. Japan could only keep to itself for so long. In 1853, American Commodore Matthew Perry boldly sailed his fleet into Tokyo Harbor. He convinced the Tokugawa shogun to open Japan's borders.

Ieyasu Tokugawa was the first Tokugawa shogun. His descendants controlled Japan for more than 200 years.

But Japan's emperor, Mutsuhito, disagreed with the shogun. On the emperor's behalf, many samurai charged into battle against the Tokugawa government. When the battle smoke cleared, the emperor was once again in control of Japan.

Samurai fought to give Emperor Mutsuhito full control of Japan.

THE SAMURAI IN TROUBLE

Many samurai hoped that Emperor Mutsuhito would return Japan to its old ways. But that was not the case. The emperor went back on his word and opened Japan's borders. He forced all daimyo and samurai to return their lands and organized a national army. The samurai had lost their jobs and their important status.

Throughout Japan, statues stand in honor of Takomori Saigo, the last samurai.

A samurai named Takamori Saigo, part of the powerful Satsuma clan, disagreed with the emperor's policies. In 1877, he banded the samurai together to fight to preserve their way of life. This battle was called the Satsuma Rebellion. There were only 20,000 brave samurai against 60,000 modern government fighters. The samurai were crushed in bitter defeat.

SAMURAI TODAY

Though the samurai warriors are gone, their spirit lives on in Japan. The code of bushido has greatly influenced Japanese people. Respect and loyalty are two of the most important values in Japanese society.

There are still honored descendants of the samurai in Japan today. Samurai warriors had a moral code as fierce as their fighting skills. These noble warriors are worthy of the world's fascination and respect.

GLOSSARY

class (KLASS)—a group of people in society with a similar way of life or range of income

daimyo (DIME-yo)—a nobleman of Japan who owned a great deal of land

descendant (di-SEND-uhnt)—a person's children and family members born after those children

martial arts (MAR-shuhl ARTS)—styles of fighting or self-defense that come from the Far East

meditate (MED-i-tayt)—to relax the mind and body by a regular program of mental exercise

privilege (PRIV-uh-lij)—a special right or advantage given to a person or a group of people

ronin (ROE-nihn)—a samurai who had left his master or whose master had died

shogun (SHOH-guhn)—a military general who once ruled Japan

READ MORE

Dean, Arlan. *Samurai: Warlords of Japan.* Way of the Warrior. New York: Children's Press, 2005.

Duey, Kathleen. *Samurai.* Time Soldiers. Carlsbad, Calif.: Big Guy Books, 2006.

Turnbull, Stephen. *Samurai Warfare.* London: Arms and Armour Press, 2002.

INTERNET SITES

FactHound offers a safe, fun way to find Internet sites related to this book. All of the sites on FactHound have been researched by our staff.

Here's how:

1. Visit *www.facthound.com*

2. Choose your grade level.

3. Type in this book ID **0736864334** for age-appropriate sites. You may also browse subjects by clicking on letters, or by clicking on pictures and words.

4. Click on the **Fetch It** button.

FactHound will fetch the best sites for you!

INDEX